Dowsing

Dowsing

With an account of some
Original Experiments by

Thomas Fiddick, J.P.

**Edited and with an Introduction by
Chris Bond**

The Cornovia Press

Introduction

The history of dowsing for minerals in Cornwall is a subject which has not received a great deal of attention over the years, although considering the superabundance of mining activity in the region it is an art which has undoubtedly witnessed a great deal of practise. The technique is believed to have been originally brought here by German miners and mineralogists in the 16th century, many of whom, with the encouragement of Elizabeth I, came to Cornwall and other parts of the British Isles in order to prospect and to aid in the exploitation and smelting of Britain's largely untapped mineral resources. Many of them settled here.

In 1556, Georgius Agricola, the German "father of mineralogy", wrote *De Re Metallica*. The book was considered to be *the* authoritative text on mining for the next two centuries. The work contains descriptions of the techniques of the German dowsers, and includes illustrations of the craft, one of which is featured on the front cover of this booklet. Over two centuries later William Pryce, the acknowledged authority on mining matters in Cornwall at that time, reported several contemporary cases of successful dowsing in Cornwall and included William Cookworthy's account of dowsing in his *Mineralogia Cornubiensis* in 1778. In Germany at this time, dowsers were held in very high regard, above that of surveyors, and mineralogical dowsers were required to have completed a diploma. It was, at the time, a well respected technique.

Dowsing for minerals once again achieved prominence in the first few decades of the 20th century when the craze surrounding the radioactive element radium took a firm hold of the public's imagination. Health products and treatments containing the element, considered a wonder drug and a cure-all, were produced in ever-increasing quantities. Mines such as South Terras near St Austell and Trenwith in St Ives were quickly put to work in procuring supplies of pitchblende and uranium, and setts for such mines were granted by the mine owners for very large sums of money.

In 1910, Sir William F. Barrett, professor of physics at the Royal College of Science in Dublin and a principal founder of the Society for Psychical Research, conducted experiments to determine whether radium salts could be detected by dowsing. But the experiment was designed to test whether or not radioactivity was the cause of the involuntary movements dowsers experienced rather than with any commercial possibilities. Such possibilities would, though, be thoroughly tested in 1914 when Professor Otto Edler von Graeve travelled to Vancouver Island in order to dowse for radium and gold on behalf of a syndicate. He had himself, the previous year, published a book on dowsing entitled *Meine Wünschelrutentätigkeit*. It was into this heavily charged atmosphere that Fiddick's pamphlet was first released, and the enthusiasm he shows for his findings is undoubtedly coloured by the possibilities promised by this brave new world.

Fiddick's pamphlet, printed by The Camborne Printing and Stationery Company, Limited, was originally published in 1913, a few years before Alfred Watkins would graft a new fork onto the history of dowsing by virtue of his seminal books on ley lines: *Early British Trackways* and *The Old Straight Track*. Watkins was to influence both the birth and the development of the modern field of earth mysteries. I would here like to extend my warm appreciation and thanks to my good friend and mentor Professor Charles Thomas for allowing me to digitise his own copy of the original pamphlet.

I have also included here, by way of an appendix, an article originally featured in *The Advertiser* newspaper, published in Adelaide in 1927, and which compliments the original text and gives details of Fiddick's later experiments in using dowsing for determining the fertility of eggs. This is of particular interest to myself, as the one notable example of my own experiments with dowsing concern my attempts to determine the number of kittens contained within the abdomen of my friend's heavily gravid cat. I had used a pendulum for the purpose, a technique which, in a similar way to Fiddick's "Dowsing Cone", produces revolutions rather than linear movements. At the time I was perplexed by the fact that the sixth revolution, always the last, seemed weaker than the rest, and so I could not decide whether five or six kittens were indicated. The cat gave birth, in my care, a few weeks later. The sixth and last kitten was stillborn.

Chris Bond

November 2011

Preface

The subject dealt with in this pamphlet is not by any means a new one. "Dowsing" or "Rhabdomancy" is "As old as the hills." In the past owing to the atmosphere of Magic and mystery surrounding it, and also to the trickery of charlatans, Dowsing as a real and practical function has often been repudiated by scientists and ascribed by them and many others to the ignorance and superstition of its votaries, and this apparently, without any serious attempt to discover whether it had a basis of fact or not. But in consequence of its persistence, and the remarkable achievements accomplished by its aid, and perhaps also to the increased desire in the present day to find the "True inwardness of things," Divining has of late been receiving more attention from the scientific world. Although manifestly presenting many difficulties, the mists enveloping it are being vigourously attacked, and not without some success. If in the following pages I am able to contribute but a single ray of light in assisting to penetrate the gloom, I shall feel compensated for my efforts.

T.F.

Beacon House, Camborne

May, 1913.

Dowsing

"DOWSING," or the means adopted for finding Minerals or Water by the aid of a Dowsing Rod or Stick, is an old practice often used by Cornishmen and others in their search for lodes or for possible springs.

Briefly, the miners' custom was to cut a forked stick shaped like the letter Y from a hazel, a white thorn, a holly, or other tree, and to hold one side of the fork in each hand, turning the projection from the two forks upwards, and then to walk very slowly over the ground to be tested. If a mineral lode or water was present, the projecting point would turn towards it.

The "Rod" in Ancient Times.

The origin of the Virgula Furcata or "Forked Twig" may be traced back to very early times. It is probably an adaption of the old "Divining Rod" Virgula Divinata used by the Ancients.

I suppose the earliest known mention of the "rod" is in Exodus, Chapter 7, verses 8 to 12:—

"And the Lord spake unto Moses and unto Aaron saying,

"When Pharaoh shall speak unto you, saying, shew a miracle for you, then thou shalt say unto Aaron, take thy

rod, and cast it before Pharaoh and it shall become a serpent."

"And Moses and Aaron went in unto Pharaoh, and they
did so as the Lord had commanded; and Aaron cast down his
rod before Pharaoh, and before his servants, and it became a
serpent."

"Then Pharaoh also called his wise men and the sorcer-
ers; now the Magicians of Egypt, they also did in like manner with their enchantments."

"For they cast down every man his rod, and they became serpents, but Aaron's rod swallowed up their rods."

"Divination by Rods" was practised by the Ancients in
the following manner:—The staff was placed upright and
then allowed to fall and the decision of the course of any
Army, etc., was according as the staff fell.

"Divination" by shooting arrows was very common.
Many arrows were shot and the march of any Army was pro-
secuted in the direction in which the greatest number fell,
or the arrows were marked with the names of devoted cities,
and that was first attacked the name of which was first
drawn. There were also other forms of "Divination."

Moses enjoined upon the Israelites abstinence from the
practice of consulting Diviners, Enchanters, etc.

The use of "Divining Arrows" is forbidden in the Koran
(the Mohammedan Bible) in the following passage:—

"Surely, O true believer, wine and images and lots and
divining arrows are an abomination of the work of Satan,
avoid them, therefore, that ye may prosper."

It is impossible to ascertain the date or to name the person who made this discovery. Agricola in his Latin Treatise *"De Re Metallica"* published in 1540, says, "That the application of the enchanted or Divining Rod to metallic matters took its rise from magicians, and the fountains of enchantment. Now the Ancients not only endeavoured to procure the necessaries of life by a divining or enchanted rod, but also to change the forms of things by the same instrument, for the magicians of Egypt as we learn from the Hebrew writings changed their rods into serpents, and in Homer Minerva turned Ulysses when old into the likeness of a young man, and again to his former appearance.

Circe also changed the companions of Ulysses into beasts, and again restored them to the human shape, and Mercury with his rod called Caduceus, gave sleep to the wakeful, and awakened those that were asleep, and hence in all probability arose the application of the forked rod to the discovery of hidden treasure."

The "Dowsing" Rod has been employed, not only in the search for minerals but also for any buried objects. In the South of France in the 17th Century it was used in tracking criminals and heretics.

Its abuse led to a decree of the inquisition in 1701, forbidding its employment for purposes of justice.

This means of discovering metalliferous lodes is said to have been introduced into Cornwall by some miners from the Hartz Mountains in Germany about 300 years ago.

Doubters.

Many able men look with little favour on "Divining," but it seems likely that in the old days lodes were frequently found by this process. Like some other systems, it is not infallible, but that it is an entire failure, must, I think, be regarded as a mistake. It is quite probable that the "rod" has been used dishonestly by many, and this coupled with the fact that it will turn to almost any mineral and also to veins containing insufficient mineral to profitably work, has often caused disappointment. When, for instance, mispickel or iron pyrites has resulted from the search instead of better paying ores, or water instead of mineral, the results have helped to discredit it.

It is very easy to ridicule "dowsing." But is it not a fact that some of our greatest discoveries have been made by men who, in their day have been laughed at for their pains? Chemistry, in a great measure, arose from alchemy, and astronomy from astrology.

The Magic of the past sometimes becomes the the Science of the present.

That "Divining" is not fully understood, goes without saying. It has always been, and yet remains, to a considerable extent, a mystery. Why does the "rod" turn in the hands of some persons, and not when held in the same manner by others? We must not refuse to give credence to the function because we are ignorant of its genesis. There are individuals who doubt almost everything. "The fool hath said in his heart there is no God."

Having been personally interested in dowsing for several years, as soon as I found that the "twig" would turn in my hands, I became more so. I have recently been carrying out a series of original experiments on this subject, and the outcome has rather surprised me. So far as is known to me, these tests have never been applied to "dowsing." They tend to prove that there is a good deal more in "Divining" than has ever been dreamt of in our philosophy, and to show "dowsing" to be a real "force."

I do not claim to explain the "why" or "wherefore" of these results, which have been achieved after many experiments, but only profess to be a learner. Personally, it is impossible at present to account with certainty for the meaning of these developments. Others more gifted than myself, may be able to do so.

The cause of the turning of the "twig" is suggested by Professor Barrett, F.R.S., a very eminent authority, to be the subconscious mind of the Dowser acting on the muscles of the arm. No one however, seems to explain with absolute assurance, what the "power" really is.

Although some authorities refuse to believe that it is the effect of Electricity, one feels persuaded that the latter is in some form, a contributing cause. It is perhaps, however, allied with another "Factor" in producing the "Dowsing" results.

A considerable number of people can 'Dowse' who are quite ignorant of their capacity in this respect. There seems to be no sex barrier here. Women can "Divine" equally as well as men. I recently met a lady who had "dowsed" at least one lode on her property, but the power is not hereditary, passing from parent to offsping. It is undoubtedly a "gift" and if a person after a proper trial, cannot successfully use the forked twig, it is unlikely that he will ever acquire the ability to do so, "Dowsers are born, not made."

The Dowser, The Forked Twig and the Mineral.

The fact of there being a connecting link between the Human Body, the wood and the mineral, can be so clearly shown as I think, to leave little room for doubt.

If I take a circular block of wood and hold a Metallic Agent over it, it will move around and around it, just as if it was a mineral substance.

As a further proof of the connection, and as evidence of the existence of this "energy," when I place a "Dowsing Rod" with the projecting end upwards on a table (keeping it securely in this position), and then hold the agent over this projecting point, it will immediately commence to rotate, but if I lay the rod flat on the table, and no point is clear from the latter, there is no such action.

Again, if one fork is held in my left hand, and the agent suspended from my right hand over the projection, the movement will take place, and when a person who cannot "Divine" holds one fork in his hand, and I hold the other in my left hand, whilst I suspend the Agent over the projecting end with my right hand, the "action" occurs, but not quite so marked as in the last experiment.

Electricity comes out at points, and in the two preceding experiments, this power does the same.

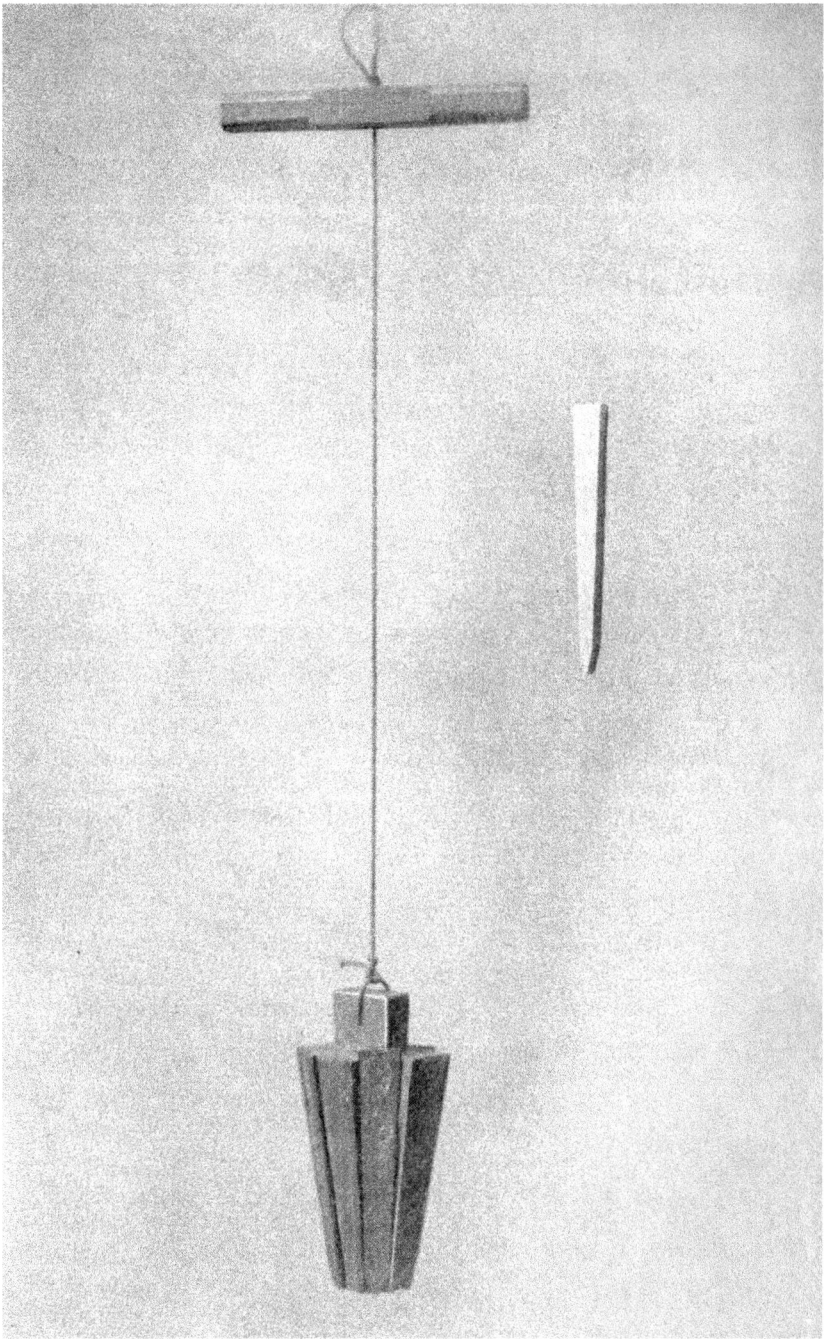

"The Dowsing Cone," invented by the author.

7

It is evident that whether the wood comes between the body and the metal (as it usually does in dowsing), or the metal comes between the body and the wood, the connection is established just the same, and with a similar result.

The "Dowsing Cone."

In pursuing my experiments, I found that 'Divining' could be accomplished with wood in quite a different form to the ordinary "Forked Twig" and after considerable reflection, I designed the "Dowsing Cone" as shewn on page 7. The movements of this are, however, very distinct from the "Turning down of the Rod." Its shape as will be seen, is that of an inverted cone (with the apex removed.) Around this are recesses for slips of various metals, or wood containing the latter, shaped similar to shields. It is suspended by a cord from a bar. In "Divining," this is held in the hand of the "Dowser" over the ground to be tested. If mineral or water is present underneath, the "Cone" will soon commence to oscillate, and continue to do so.

I have never yet held it a sufficient time for it to cease. Possibly the oscillation would continue as long as my strength permitted me to hold it. (In the case of the "Rod" it is a mere momentary "Downward turn," or perhaps some tremulous motions.)

It is a very simple movement, and yet a very singular and mysterious one as to its cause, and although I have made the "test" on very many occasions, it has never once failed to "act."

Like the "Dowsing Rod," there is no response whatever, if held by some persons in the same manner, and it appears to "act" only now and again with others.

The "power" which produces this movement will appear so remote and inexplicable to many people that they will not readily believe it to be caused by any other agency than the premeditated action of the demonstrator. There seems to be no doubt that it is the same "force" which affects the "Divining Rod."

A hundred and one questions will suggest themselves with regard to this movement, some of which it may be possible to answer. Here let me apologise for the frequent use of the personal pronoun by observing that as most of these experiments are original, it could scarcely be avoided.

It can be demonstrated that the "energy" or "power" created by this method will take a right angle action and also a circular motion, according to circumstances, but not a triangular movement.

One hand only is used in this system, and if whilst the "Cone" is in motion, I take a mineral in my other hand, the action gradually lessens, and at last entirely ceases, but if I grasp a piece of glass in the left hand, it will not stop it. Particulars respecting the use of Metals with the "Dowsing Cone" are given under "Dowsing Assay."

The Direction of the Lode.

It is noteworthy that the movement of the "Cone" is usually along the line of the "lode," although at first it may not follow the correct course; in a minute or two it will generally change, and oscillate along the direction of the latter. This will be found useful, as shewing the direction of the mineral vein under that particular spot, and can be exhibited by placing a block of metal lengthways at right angles with the body, when it will move to and fro at right angles with the body over the mineral. Now exactly reverse the position of the metal or mineral and the "cone" will very soon alter its course, and commence and continue to swing the long way of the latter.

I believe this system of "Divining" to be much more sensitive to minerals than the ordinary rod. It is surprising how small a quantity of metal will effect the "Dowsing Cone." A speck of gold not larger than the head of a pin will cause it to oscillate and to continue the motion. Very small pieces of Copper, Lead, Tin, &c., will effect it in a like manner. It must be remembered that the "Cone" can only be utilized by a person who has the "gift" and is not of itself a "Dowser" but only an "Agent."

Different Effects on Different Individuals.

The action of the "Forked Twig" varies considerably. In the case of some "Dowsers" it is much more marked than in that of others, who possess the "gift." It seems almost to electrify them. Then there are many people in whose hands the "Rod" will turn now and again over a mineral, but not every time they hold it; the latter are uncertain, and therefore poor "Dowsers." An illustration of its powerful effect once came under my own notice. I placed the "Twig" in the hands of an individual who had a metallic substance put on a table in front of him, and he had not held it for more than a few moments before the "Rod" began to quiver violently and it affected him so much that he commenced to lift his toes up and down from the floor, and then began to dance on his heels so rapidly that one would have thought it almost impossible. He went from one end of the room to the other, beating the floor with his heels almost with the rapidity of a pneumatic stamps, and then sank into an arm chair nearly exhausted. It seemed to have affected his heart very much, but he said that the first effect produced was most exhilarating, and that he felt as if new life was entering his body. I repeated this experiment with him once or twice after, with similar results, but did not allow him to hold the "rod" so long, as I was afraid of its influence on his heart. One has heard of its very powerful effect on others, but cases of this kind are of course, quite abnormal.

A "Diviner" who read an article of mine on this subject, has sent the following interesting account of his experiences:—

1. Strange to relate, the "rod" works with me in quite the opposite way. I hold it down <u>and it turns up</u>.

2. If I hold it the reverse way, viz. up, it refuses to work. This I suppose in some way creates a negative.

3. Or if I walk backwards and hold the "Rod" the same way as I usually do, viz. <u>down,</u> it will not act? Another negative.

4. But if I use the two negatives (as I call them) it appears to create a positive, and the rod then acts just as freely, but in the opposite direction! Can you explain this?

This gentleman has given me a "poser" but although I may not be able to give a satisfactory reply to his question I can assure him that his is not an isolated instance of the "Twig" turning upwards. There are others who hold the "Rod" down instead of up, and in Dowsing it turns up instead of <u>down</u> as is generally the case.

Electricity is sometimes peculiar in its movements, and so is the "Dowsing Rod." Time and patient study will perhaps reveal the cause of these eccentricities.

A very interesting and instructive old work by Mr. Williams Price of Redruth, entitled "Mineralogia Corunbiensis" and published in 1778, contains a chapter on "Dowsing" and in his preface he says "The merit of the essay, *i.e.* the chapter on the Virgula Divinatoria is due to Mr. William Cookworthy of Plymouth." This was the same gentleman who in about the year 1755 discovered the use of Kaolin or China Clay as a producer of Porcelain, a process for the manufacture of which he patented in 1768 and thus became the pioneer of the vast China Clay trade in Cornwall and Devon.

The Virtues of the "Rod."

Pryce says—"Though the virtues of the rod may not be easily allowed by the incredulous, yet for my own part, I want no further evidence of its properties than I have already obtained, to fix my opinion of its virtues, at least the memoir is curious and the subject deserves to be enquired into." He quotes instances of the successful use of the "Rod" in finding mineral.

How to Use the Rod.

First cut your "Rod" from a White Thorn or Hazel Tree. As both these are plentiful, the former especially so, this will be a simple matter (almost any tree will do). The second year's growth of wood is said to be preferable. It should be shaped like the letter "Y".

Careful search amongst the small branches of the Tree, will soon reveal a suitable "Twig." It need not be a large one, and can easily be obtained by cutting off the branch about three inches inside the two forks. This will form the project-ing end of the "Rod." Then trim off the leaves.

Grasp one fork in each hand with the palms upwards, keeping the elbows close to the sides, and turn the project-ing end up, still keeping the palms upwards. The position of the "rod" will then resemble the letter "Y" reversed, thus, "ʎ" and hold it as tightly in the hands as possible (when I first tried it, I held it loosely thinking that it would not move if grasped firmly, but I soon discovered that the tight-er I held it, the more it would try to turn).

If the holder has the "gift" and he is over water or a mineral Lode, it will almost immediately commence to turn towards it.

A detailed statement on the manner of using the "Rod" is given by Pryce. He says:—"Walk steadily and slowly on with it, and a person that hath been accustomed to carry it, will meet with a single repulsion and attraction, every 3, 4, or 5 yards, which must not be heeded, it being only from the water that is between every bed of Killas, Grouan, or other strata. When the holder approaches a Lode so near as its semi-diameter, the Rod feels loose in the hands and is very sensibly repelled towards the face, if it is thrown back so far as to touch the hat, it must be brought forward to its usual elevation, when it will continue to be repelled till the foremost foot is over the edge of the Lode, when this is the case, if the rod is held well, there will first be a small repulsion towards the face, but this is momentary and the rod will be immediately drawn irresistibly down, and will continue to be so in the whole passage over the Lode; but as soon as the foremost foot is beyond its limits, the attraction from the hindmost foot, which is still on the Lode, or else the repulsion on the other side, or both, throw the rod back toward the face.

The distance from the point where the attraction began, and where it ended, is the breath of the lode, or rather, of a horizonal section of the bryle or back just under the earth.

We must then turn, and trace it on obliquely or in the way of Zig-zag, as far as may be thought necessary.

In the course of this tracing a lode, all the circumstances of it, as far as they relate to its back, will be discovered, as its breadth at different places, its being squeezed together by hard strata, its being cut off and thrown aside from the regular course by a cross-gossan, etc.

In order to determine this, it will be necessary that someone present should either cut up a turf, or place a stone at the places where the rod began, and on the other side where it ceased to be attracted. If the Rod is well held, its motion is surprisingly quick and lively. Nothing is necessary, but to keep the mind indifferent, to grasp the rod pretty strongly and steadily, opening the hands, and raising the rod with the middle fingers, every time it is drawn down.

If the rod is raised and replaced without opening the hands, it will not work."

Divining for Water.

It often happens that there is a scarcity of water on an estate, a good supply of which, if found, would prove to be a boon to the proprietor or his tenants. The question naturally arises whether there are springs beneath the surface, and if so, where they are located.

The geologist is frequently called in and consulted. On other occasions the "Dowser's" aid is sought. The former sometimes gives valuable advice, but in certain cases, after expensive borings have been made in the places selected by him, no water has been discovered. Then the "Dowser's" advice has been sought, and a copious supply of the precious liquid has been found, in fact the results have often proved that it would have been much wiser, and more economical, to have first called in the aid of the "Forked Twig."

But in neighbourhoods which are highly mineralized a difficulty often arises from the fact of the "Rod" turning to a mineral just as it turns to water; the search might therefore result in finding a "solid" instead of a "liquid."

Some persons claim to know whether the Twig is turning to water or to mineral, but it seems to be a very doubtful claim. I believe, however, that I have discovered a method of "Divining" which will distinguish between the two. In dowsing for water, care should be taken to sink exactly under the spot indicated, because it is often the case that the water flows through, or is contained in a "fissure," and by going to the right or left only a very short distance, the water will be missed and disappointment will be the result. This precaution would also be necessary where the soil is composed of clay, which holds water very "snugly."

A correspondent, (a Clergyman) from a distance, has written giving me this interesting account of his experiences as a "Water Finder," it shows what obstinacy can do.

1. I located a spring for a Farm and told the owner, he would know the spot, as it was immediately opposite a certain large bush in the hedge, and was exactly 11 yards from it. What was my surprise one day to find the owner at my door with a wagonette, and not at all in a good humour. He told me that "He never had any faith in a "Divining Rod" and now had found it to be a perfect fraud, etc". I went over to the spot with him, and then found that the well sinker had on his own responsibility sunk elsewhere, not many yards away, it is true, but far enough to miss the water which ran in a straight line across the field. He then bored at the right spot and found the water, and when they sunk the well, the men had to make a bolt, for it came in with such a force, that it shot up the well for several feet. The men having driven an iron bar down "to see if there was any water."!

2. I was asked to "Divine" for a supply for a mansion. I located a spot, but it was unfortunately just in the centre of the carriage drive, which by the way, was

not finished, and could quite easily have been diverted. The sinker, thinking that "a few yards would not make any difference," sunk elsewhere, and having sunk for a considerable depth, the builder came over to see me in a 'stew.' I went with him, and tried the "rod" again, it still worked on the old spot. I suggested that they should drive a tunnel to the spot—Result—found plenty of water, and have never been without since.

3. A town was short of water, I heard they were going to bore by steam. I walked across with the "Rod" and said to one of the leading men that there was no water there. His reply was they had had the Government geologist down, and an engineer, and they said there was a water bearing strata at 150 feet. Well they bored 300 feet and drove in steel tubes and never found any water, they next bored another field by hand, I told them there was none there. They bored 150 feet, and not finding any, retired. Hundreds of pounds being thrown away.

The experiences here narrated could be multiplied over and over again as proof of the effectiveness of the "Divining Rod" in finding water. Similar results have happened in many parts of this and other countries. Professor Sir W. F. Barrett, F.R.S., (previously alluded to,) has made a large number of exhaustive tests as to the utility of the "Rod" for this purpose.

In a pamphlet entitled "The history and mystery of the Divining Rod," he gives some truly remarkable and well authenticated cases of water finding by this means.

"Dowsing Assay."

Probably the title of this chapter will appear to be somewhat sensational, but, "Truth is sometimes stranger than Fiction."

In "Divining" a mineral will not 'act' on its like. This fact proves to be very valuable, for, by its means I think that it will often be possible to ascertain the particular kind of mineral beneath the surface, and moreover without digging for it. It would of course, be wise to first find out whether any mineral is present, and this could be done by carefully testing the ground with the "Dowsing Cone" which will oscillate when over mineral, on the latter being discovered, a metal shield should be inserted in a recess of the "Cone" and if there is no oscillation when held over the same spot, the same kind of metal (or ore from which it is obtained,) is probably underneath. The trial should be continued by placing other metals in the "Cone" to ascertain whether any other mineral or minerals are present. This system will also be useful in finding out the metallic contents of any given substance. I have, on several occasions, discovered the contents of stones, which have either been picked up by myself, or handed to me by some other person, the results having afterwards been verified by either chemical or vanning assay. This is the most speedy method I know of. Ore bodies which would take an ordinary assayer a considerable time to test, occupy by this system but a few minutes only, entail scarcely any trouble, and will, according to my experience, be generally correct. (Whilst going to press I am hopeful of having found a new process (by "Divining") of verifying the "Dowsing Assay" just alluded to.)

Is it Electricity?

Several of my experiments appear to suggest that it is a form of Electrical Energy.

A piece of note paper placed between the mineral "dowsed" and the "Cone" will prevent oscillation. Now, if I use friction over one side of the paper, and put it on the mineral with the rubbed side upwards, and again suspend the "Cone" over it, the "action" occurs, but when the rubbed side is turned down, *i.e.* on the mineral, it will fail to respond. If the surface of the "Cone" be rubbed briskly, and it is immediately after suspended over the mineral, there is no movement whatever.

On the contrary when the surface of vulcanite or glass is rubbed, the same "motion" can be produced as if they were minerals.

Several years ago it was demonstrated that living tissues gave forth Electric Currents. Recently when discussing the subject of this pamphlet with a friend who happened to be an Electrician I remarked that I could generate Electricity, a statement which he gravely doubted, but in order to ascertain its truth, or otherwise, he connected me with a Galvanometer and found a very distinct effect on the needle. He then declared that he was absolutely convinced of the accuracy of my contention. By placing common salt in a basin of water connected with the Galvanometer, and holding my clenched fists in it, the power was increased.

Conductors and Non-Conductors.

As to conductors and non-conductors, this "force" will pass through many feet of earth, slate more than an inch thick, several inches of cement concrete, or clothing or wood of a considerable thickness. I find that this "power" will also pass through a human being. All the above are conductors. It will not however, penetrate a single sheet of note paper, sheet lead, porcelain, wax, vulcanite, or glass. These latter articles are non-conductors. It might be mentioned that the conductors and non-conductors of electricity seem to be almost, if not, quite, synonymous with the conductors and non-conductors of this "force," and that after friction, as in the case of electricity, the non-conductors become conductors, which is rather suggestive.

A short time ago I was asked whether the "Divining Rod" would "act" if the "Dowser" was insulated from the ground beneath him. I have since ascertained this by standing on a sheet of Asbestos (the latter resting on Glass Jars) with mineral placed under the sheet, thus being completely insulated. In this position the "Twig" would not make the slightest movement, but immediately the Asbestos was removed, and I stood over the same mineral, it acted vigorously.

Whilst there are some features of this "energy" closely approximating to Electricity, one differentiates it from the latter with regard to outside surfaces.

Electricity is said to be attracted by the outside surface of certain substances, but I ascertain in "Divining" with a mineral, that although the surface of a metal may be coated or effectually covered with another metal that the inside metal will stop the usual movement. Thus in dowsing on Tin plate (which is Iron with a Tin coating or veneer) with an Iron "Shield" in the "Cone," the latter will not act in the slightest manner, in this way shewing the presence of Iron although enveloped with the Tin coating. It is quite possible that there may be some explanation of this not antagonistic to Electricity.

A rather amusing incident occurred recently. A young friend of mine was persuaded by his Hair Dresser to try Electric Massage. He had the massage applied; and within an hour afterwards, saw me, and knowing my interest in "Divining" jocularly requested me to try my "Dowsing Cone" on his locks. I readily consented, and found that the "Cone" when held over his head became most active, moving about in a lively manner, just as it would do on a very sensitive mineral. As a further trial I placed my left hand between it, and my friend's hair, this produced a considerable tingling sensation in my hand, which extended to the arm, but caused the oscillation to cease.

The "Dowsing Rod" was also held over his head, and was strongly affected, immediately turning down toward it. The next day I saw him again, and made exactly similar tests, but these produced no response whatever, thus showing that the Electricity had gone from his hair. Although this incident has its comical side, it may possibly be accepted as additional evidence of the influence of Electricity in causing both the movement of the "Rod" and the "Cone."

The Remarkable Effect of Colour in "Divining."

An Electric Current proceeding from the Human Body is said to be affected by the colour of the light under which it is emitted, a yellow light causing a considerable increase in its activity, and a red light being nearly as strong.

I have discovered that in "Dowsing" there is a somewhat similar effect, (supporting the theory that Electricity is at any rate a "partner in the concern.")

Glass, as previously stated is a non-conductor of the "Divining Force." An ordinary glass jar placed over a metal will prevent any movement of the "Cone," but if a ruby tinted glass jar is inverted and placed over a copper disc, the "Cone" when held above it, immediately begins to rotate, proving the powerful action of the red light. But more than this, a sheet of glass or a piece of paper, put over the disc, and under the inverted "ruby" jar are (contrary to the usual course) penetrated by the "power" and the "Cone" is set in motion.

Another experiment has elucidated something else. I again placed the inverted Red Jar over the Copper Disc, this time putting the paper outside, and on the top of the Jar, and found that the "Cone" was quite motionless, which probably shows that in "Divining" the "power" starts from the "Dowser" and not from the mineral below the surface. Electricity also "plays" towards the earth!

Magnetic Effect.

The effect of a magnet on the "Cone" is very marked. It will prevent any movement whatever.

In addition to the deterrent effect of magnetic power, any of the substances which I have found to be non-conductors, would, if coming between the rod and a mineral lode, prevent its "action." As a trial, I recently spread a newspaper on the surface under which I had "dowsed" a lode. Holding the rod over the newspaper, it failed to budge an inch.

If one had not previously known the influence of paper so placed, one would undoubtedly have said that there was no mineral under that particular spot.

Strange to say, this force can be transmitted. I have succeeded in transferring my power to another person who is not able to "dowse," and to cause him to do so; and yet a person who cannot "dowse" can prevent me from doing it.

Some Minerals which do not appear to cause oscillation.

There are some minerals, which, contrary to the general rule fail to produce the usual movement of the "Dowsing Cone." When held over Magnetic Iron Ore, the "Cone" remains perfectly still.

Mercury also fails to create any motion, Aluminium (Commercial) has no effect. This usually contains Silicon which may interfere with its conductivity of Electricity.

Then again there is that remarkable mineral Pitchblende, from which Radium is obtained. This being a powerful substance, one naturally thought that it would make the "Cone" exceedingly lively, but to my surprise it did not move and was as "Idle as a painted ship upon a painted ocean" even when the whole of the following metals:— Gold, Silver, Copper, Tin, Lead, and Zinc were placed in a heap with Pitchblende on the top, no vibration occurred. The Pitchblende simply mastered the lot! But I was not then aware of the fact that Uranium Compounds caused the air near them to be a conductor of Electricity. If a small quantity of an ore of Uranium be placed in proximity to a charged Gold Leaf Electroscope, the latter rapidly loses its charge. This property of Pitchblende (an ore of Uranium) appears to rob metals of their electricity and thus dissipates the "Dowsing" Force. I have ascertained that this peculiarity can be overcome and a fairly strong "swing" of the "Cone" be obtained, thus providing a "Test" for its presence in any substance.

Breaking the Circuit.

In suspending the "Cone" over a metal with the right hand, it forms a circuit between my body and the metal, and as a result, commences to oscillate. Now, if, whilst it is in motion I point to it with the left index finger (or hand) the oscillation very speedily slackens and then ceases.

Very likely this effect is caused by the circuit being broken. When held in the same manner over a magnet there is no "action," but by pointing to it with my left finger (as in the former case) the movement almost instantly begins by the "Cone" oscillating towards the finger, which it will follow in any direction and towards any point. In this instance, a circuit seems to be set up independent of the magnet.

The Practical Advantages of Dowsing.

Dowsing for minerals in Cornwall has for many years almost gone into disuetude.

There are probably several reasons for this, but it occurs to me that one may have been largely responsible, viz :- That a great number of mineral properties having been discovered and worked, some of them again and again after longer or shorter intervals (owing to the fluctuations in the price of metals, or the poverty of the Lodes) has prevented that very considerable amount of surface search or "costeaning" formerly engaged in for new properties, in which the "Divining Rod" played such a preliminary and important function.

Of late years the custom has often been to re-work old and frequently water-logged mines which entailed heavy pumping charges before any mineral could be returned, instead of endeavouring to discover mineral nearer the surface for which "Dowsing" is so serviceable.

It may perhaps surprise some folks to learn that there are about 500 disused mines in the County of Cornwall. Some of these have provided "Hunting Ground" time after time for mining men, but not in all cases of a happy sort.

It is unquestionable that a vast amount of mineral still lies undiscovered in this County, and elsewhere, and awaiting the effort of man to turn it to account. In this particular work "Dowsing" might be found most useful.

Pryce says:—"If the lode is alive to its top, or as it is usually phrased by the Tinners, to grass; more work may be done in the way of discovery with the "rod" in a quarter of an hour, than by the usual method in months, as a person has nothing to do, but to open the lode immediately at grass, and discover its size and underlie, which may be done at a trifling expense." It might also be utilized in tracing a lode which has been productive in one mine, through virgin ground in its proximity when a few costean pits would possibly reveal a paying proposition.

Nothing has been said as to the employment of this "Means" underground. It might prove to be of much utility in many cases.

Unlike "Dowsing" for mineral, "Dowsing" for water is still practised rather extensively in some places, and with very successful results.

On the score of economy of time, capital and labour, it often possesses very distinct advantages. Ignorance and prejudice have however, sometimes combined to prevent its use.

Influence of Will Power on the "Dowsing Cone."

At the close of an address on "Divining," I was asked whether this subject had any connection with "Table Turning" and I replied that I hardly knew whether it had or had not. Since then, further experience has shewn me that "Will Power" or some other Psychic Force exerts an influence on the "Dowsing Cone" if held over a metal. For instance, by commanding it to cease oscillating, the movement stops entirely. If it is travelling in one direction, by "willing" it to swing another way, it gradually ceases its first movement and oscillates in the direction "willed"; but when using one hand only, unless held over a metal, no "Will Power" which I possess can make it move. This tends to prove that metals have a very decided influence, hence the "Dowsing" effect.

"Divining" Telepathy.

To carry it still further, if when holding the "Cone" in my right hand, another person clasps my left hand, it is almost invariably possible for him by the exercise of his "will" to alter its "swing" subject only to my remaining in a passive state during the experiment, and, stranger yet, when there is no visible contact between the second person and myself, he is able when standing several feet away to deflect the normal "movement."

In neither of the last two cases, although able to alter the motion, can the second person be sure of changing the oscillation in the direction which he desires, but he nearly always appears to "act" as a disturbing influence. Seeing that the "mind" has such a powerful "control" it does not seem unreasonable to infer that Public Competitions, Demonstrations, etc., by "Diviners" are very likely to mislead, especially in the case of persons who are of a nervous temperament, also of those easily excited. They are also liable to unjustly prejudice the public against "Dowsing."

Why is another person by clasping my hand and mentally expressing a "wish" able to deflect the "Cone"? When I commenced these investigations the thought of "Psychic

Force" or control did not appeal to me, but one feels bound to admit that the "Divining Power" can be placed under some amount of restraint, and it emphazises the importance when "Dowsing" of acting upon the advice of the Early "Diviners" by keeping the mind perfectly cool and indifferent as to what may happen. (One might add that with the ordinary "Dowsing Rod" it would be quite impossible to <u>perform many of these tests</u>.)

The "Divining Influence" without the presence of Metals or Water.

Given certain conditions the "Force" may be demonstrated in the absence of Water or Metals. This fact, as the reader will perceive, detracts in no way from the usefulness of "Dowsing" as a means of discovering Minerals, Water, or Mineral Oils.

If I suspend the "Cone" by the right hand, and point to it with the left index finger, it (the Cone) will at once begin to oscillate (just as when over a metal). In this case a circuit is apparently formed by the body of the operator, instead of being formed in the usual way, namely, by the body and the metallic substance. Not only does the movement occur in this manner, but similarly as when Metal is employed it can be controlled by the "Will" and made to oscillate in several directions.

The "Power" exerted by the "Dowser" in the experiments just alluded to, and also in ordinary "Divining," appears to be electricity, but there may be an additional factor involved.

28

The Sub-conscious Mind.

Human Personality is greater than we have ever imagined. It embraces powers that cannot be analysed by the Chemist, or demonstrated by the Physiologist. There is a "something" in man which Materialism cannot account for. Although generally supposed to be mostly in a dormant state, it probably exerts a powerful influence in the world, and has done all through the past ages. It is a mysterious and subtle faculty which Psychologists term The Sub-conscious Mind or Subliminal Self, and is thought by many to be sometimes controlled by "suggestion" from the "Will" or Conscious Mind. Is it possible that the Sub-conscious mind acts in "Divining" as a stimulus or excitant to the electricity, and causes the "Turning of the Rod," and the "Oscillation of the Dowsing Cone"? which latter movement can be dominated by the "Will" (or conscious mind) of the Dowser. The "Subliminal Self" is at present little understood, and possibly acts in many unknown and unrecognised ways, and when in unfettered activity it is perhaps the cause of a very considerable proportion of cases which are termed supernatural phenomena. This is a very fascinating subject and presents a field of enquiry, which, though admittedly difficult, may in the future produce a rich harvest of results, unlocking some of the mysteries of life, and possibly also of death and the hereafter. In this connection let me say that we are very much indebted to the Society for Psychical Research, for their patient investigation of this and kindred subjects.

Conclusion.

As the preceding investigations have been conducted solely by myself, it must not be assumed that the "conclusions" are infallibly correct.

Numerous other interesting experiments relating to this subject might have been referred to. It is permissable to add that these "tests" are very exhausting physically, and would probably be injurious if continually persisted in. It is indeed true of these that "much study is a weariness of the flesh."

Many have no faith in "Dowsing." Some people believe in scarcely anything they see or hear; no evidence appeals to them, "They would not believe though one rose from the dead."

On the other hand, there are many, who are so superstitious that they are quite prepared to believe anything and everything that they are told, and are constantly on the lookout for signs and wonders. The peculiarity of each class is carefully avoided by the genuine searcher after truth, who endeavours to steer a middle course between the Scylla of the one, and the Charybdis of the other. Whatever the "Divining Power" may be, one cannot help thinking that "Dowsing" possesses many practical advantages, and should be employed much more frequently than it is at present. Although we cannot say with certainty what the "Force" really is, our ignorance in this respect ought not to prevent our utilizing the "Power" in the public interest. What is Electricity? What is Magnetism? Probably the ablest Electrician in England is unable to fully explain either. To use a homely illustration, how many people are there who refuse to travel by an Electric Tramcar because they do not understand its motive power, or its mechanism? They simply board the car, and they reach their destination. Just so, with the "Dowser." He is seeking Water or Mineral. He walks over the ground with the "Rod." It turns to the earth. He digs a pit, and discovers a bubbling spring or a mineralised vein.

Appendix

THE DOWSING CONE.

CORNISH DISCOVERY.
"CAMBORNE SITTING ON BANK OF ENGLAND."

An important paper on "An Hour with a Dowser" was read by Mr. Thomas Fiddick, of Camborne, at a meeting of the Cornish Institute of Engineers at Camborne School of Mines. Mr. Maurice Gregory (president) presided.

In the course of his paper, illustrated with original experiments, Mr. Fiddick (reports the "West Briton") spoke of dowsing as the means adopted for finding mineral water by the aid of a forked twig. Many people believed divining to be a fraud, and some scientists labelled it a delusion. A considerable number of people to-day possessed the ability but were in complete ignorance of the fact. Dowsing was said to have been introduced into Cornwall about 300 years ago by some miners from the Hartz mountains of Germany. The instrument generally used by the diviner—a forked twig—grew on every hedgerow, and could be cut and adapted for its purpose in five minutes. The rod was grasped firmly in both hands and held firmly in an up-right position, and when held over water or a mineral vein it would turn towards it. He had evolved a differently shaped medium, also of wood, which worked in quite another way to the

32

twig and had certain advantages over it. His instrument was named the "dowsing cone," and when held over a cone or circular piece of metal it would rotate. He once caused a movement of the cone when it was held in a man's hand in a house at the other end of the street, each being invisible to the other. Here, then, they had himself as a transmitting station, the holder of the cone as a receiving station, and the cone as a recording station.

Results Twelve Miles Distant.

Since that time he had tried to cause certain movements of the cone held in the hand of a friend at Truro, who could not dowse, whilst he (Mr. Fiddick) held another cone in Camborne. A word of four letters was used and the cone stopped for two minutes between each letter. He succeeded in communicating the first three letters correctly. His friend was quite ignorant of the movements which he intended to cause, and when he brought back the diagram and compared it with the diagram prepared by him it showed that three movements out of four were right.

The lecturer referred to testing the radio-activity of minerals by the cone and said that in experimenting with radium ore one had found the test for the presence of radio-activity in a specimen of ore was by placing a piece of copper wire on a long table and putting on one end of it copper and on the other end the mineral. When the cone was held over it the cone would rotate. When pitchblende was used on the other end of the wire the cone would stop rotating. Mr. Davison, of the Camborne School of Mines, tested several specimens which were previously tried by dowsing, by a goldleaf electroscope and practically every one was proved to be correct.

In dowsing for minerals or water the conscious will was not exerted in any way. The dowser adopted a passive state of mind and unconcernedly awaited the issue. Experience had shown him that the conscious will, when asserted, mastered and controlled the diving force. For instance, when he held the cone over metal and it oscillated in the usual manner, on commanding it to stop the movement ceased entirely. Many people who possessed the power of control could not dowse. It was, however, quite possible for persons, by exercise of their will, to cause the rod to turn in the absence of both mineral and water and thus appear to be able to divine. Ignorance of those facts, not only by the public, but often by dowsers, must undoubtedly be connected with many of the disappointments attached to its practice. These experiments showed how easy it was to deceive and be deceived. In genuine dowsing a man willingly surrendered his conscious mind to the dowsing influence and simply registered the result.

Influence of Eggs.

Perhaps one of the most curious facts respecting the cone was the influence of eggs on its movements. Over some the cone oscillated, whilst with others it caused a circular action. Another peculiarity was that when the cone was held over the eggs which caused the oscillating effect, if a male person took hold of his (the speakers) left hand the motion ceased, but when suspended above the egg producing the circular motion, the cone did not stop, but continued to rotate as before, and vice-versa in the case of a female holding his left hand. If he placed the oscillating egg by the side of the one that gave the circular movement, the cone would not set, but if two circular eggs were put together the cone rotated. The question arose as to whether these effects were caused by the contents or the shell. He had found that the shell alone created no action whatever, and he concluded that the contents were responsible. He experimented again with nine eggs in succession, but the cone would only act over six. He was rather inclined to believe that the reason was that the live germ in the egg caused the movement and that those which produced no movement had either not been fertilised at all or were not sufficiently fertilised to affect the cone. In support of the theory he discovered that the eggs taken from pens in which no male bird was kept also failed to act on the cone and that eggs which produced a distinct movement had, after being boiled, or subjected to the opposite extreme of excessive cold water, became likewise impotent.

The president remarked that more prospecting was wanted in Cornwall and the use of the dowsing rod was, in his opinion, admirably adapted for preliminaries.

Experiments at Truro.

Mr. J. H. Hart stated that he had been using the dowsing rod for 20 years and in not a single instance had he failed. He had recently been engaged by Truro Water Company to explore by means of a dowsing rod the possibility of augmenting the sources of the city's water supply and if his tests were accurate and were acted upon he thought Truro would possess more water than it would know what to do with. In his opinion dowsing was essential to the location of a water supply or mineral deposits.

Mr. James Wickett said he was a strong believer in dowsing. There was no question that Cornwall was one of the most highly mineralised parts of the world, and in going over the

Duchy with dowsing appliances he had convinced himself of the truth of this statement and of the great possibilities of development Cornwall still possessed. Camborne in its poverty was literally sitting on the Bank of England. He had satisfied himself by dowsing that there was more mineral in Dolcoath Mine than had ever been taken out, and the same thing was true of other parts of the district.

This article originally featured in *The Advertiser*, Adelaide, Australia, Wednesday, November 30th, 1927.